Holiday HA-HA'S CHRISTMAS JOKES + RIDDLES

LIBRARY O LAUGHS

Dedicated to

with deep thanks for the wonderful gift
he's given me—a dream come true!

ISBN 0-8431-0469-4
A B C D E F G H I J

Holiday HA-HA'S

CHRISTMAS JOKES + RIDDLES

CRAIG YOE

LIBRARY O' LAUGHS

PSS!
PRICE STERN SLOAN

Candy canes, not coal, to: Jon Anderson, Kelli Chipponeri, AnnMarie Harris, Mara Conlon, Jayne Antipow, Joy Court, Rosalie Lent, Rebecca Goldberg, and, of course, Clizia Gussoni.

try to keep my sense of humor—even though I've never gotten anything but coal for Christmas.

So, I'm passing along this book of jokes I've come up with to create holiday cheer.

Yoe-Ho-Ho!

Craig Yoe

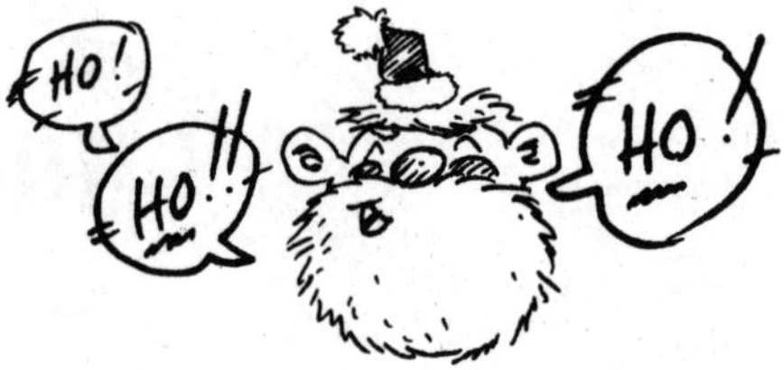
HO!
HO!!
HO!

What does a rabbit string up to decorate his Christmas tree?

—Hop-corn!

WHAT'S THOUGHTFUL AND FROZEN AND GOES, "DRIP, DRIP"?

—NICE-ICLES!

WHAT SONG DO YOU SING TO THE CHRISTMAS TREE?

-"FIR HE'S A JOLLY GOOD FELLOW!"

What do you call a really good Christmas?

-A Cool Yule!

What do you call a crab that gives presents to good boys and girls?

-Sandy Claws!

WACKY WINTER!

Why did the kids go skiing on their winter vacation?

-It was the last resort!

What is a boat's favorite Christmas carol?

—"Dock the Halls!"

How did the boy feel when he got a watch for Christmas?

—He was all wound up!

What do you call Santa when he has a pocket full of change?

–Saint Nickel-as!

How did the snowman break his leg?

–Snowfall!

What do you call a wise shovel?

–A s-know shovel!

WHAT DO PEOPLE WHO WORK ON WALL STREET LOVE MOST ABOUT CHRISTMAS?

–THE STOCK-INGS!

SNOWFALL
+ CHINESE COOKING
———————————
SHOVEL THE WOK!

What does a singer cover his presents with?

—Rapping paper!

What does Santa Claus eat at a Mexican restaurant?

-Chimney-chongas!

Why is a foot like a present?

-Because it's a stocking stuffer!

What superhero goes around presents?

-Ribbon the Boy Wonder!

Which day of the year is Prancer's favorite?

-New Deer's Eve!

WHICH REINDEER IS THE STUPIDEST?

–DUNCE-ER!

What happened when the electric train that goes around the Christmas tree got sick?

–It went "ah-choo choo!"

What is red and white and rises in the east?

–Sun-ta!

WHICH OF SANTA'S REINDEER LIVES WITH OTHER ANIMALS?

–ZOO-PID!

What's purple and sticky and goes, "Ho, ho, ho"?

–Jelly Old Saint Nick!

Stan: How far is it to the North Pole?
Jan: It's not very fa-la-la-la-la-la-la-la-la!

What is a snowman's favorite baseball position?

—Frost base!

WHAT WILL HAPPEN IF YOU'RE NAUGHTY BEFORE CHRISTMAS?

—YULE BE SORRY!

Who has antlers, pulls Santa's sleigh, and works as a plumber?

—A Drain-deer!

Which Christmas carol never gets sung?
—The Second Noel!

Why is a foot like a present?

−Because it's a stocking stuffer!

What happened when Santa got a sore throat before Christmas?

−He had to have his tinsels taken out!

Why did the turkey turn down the dessert at the Christmas dinner?

 -Because it was stuffed!

WACKY WINTER!

What does Frankenstein wear around his neck in winter?

 -A scar-f!

What do small red
fruits say to each other
on December 25th?

—"Cherry Christmas!"

ROPE
+ DECEMBER 24TH
THE KNOT BEFORE CHRISTMAS!

Why does Santa wear
suspenders?

—To keep his pants up!

What instrument did the bird play at the Christmas concert?

–The flew-t!

WHAT IS A FARMER'S FAVORITE CHRISTMAS CAROL?

–"I'M DREAMING OF A WHEAT CHRISTMAS!"

What is a playing card's favorite Christmas carol?

–"Deck the Halls!"

WHAT IS A BOXER'S FAVORITE CHRISTMAS DESSERT?

—MINCEMEAT PIE!

Where does a rocket scientist kiss her boyfriend?

–Under the missle-toe!

Why couldn't Dasher go out and play?

—Because of rain, dear!

Which day of the year is a tree's favorite?

–Christmas Leave!

HAPPY NEW YEAR

What does a cow say on January 1st?

–"Happy Moo Year!"

What do lizards say to each other on January 1st?

–"Happy Newt Year!"

What does a ghost say on January 1st?

–"Happy Boo Year!"

What does a dove say on January 1st?

–"Happy Coo Year!"

What does an owl say on January 1st?

–"Happy Whooo Year!"

What does a detective say on January 1st?

—"Happy Clue Year!"

What does a British bathroom say on January 1st?

—"Happy Loo Year!"

What does a buffalo say on January 1st?

—"Happy Gnu Year!"

What does a lawyer say on January 1st?

—"Happy Sue Year!"

What song does Dracula sing on New Year's Eve?

—"Auld Fang Syne!"

What song does a telephone sing on New Year's Eve?

—"Auld Rang Syne!"

WHAT DOES A TROUT USE TO BLOW ITS NOSE WHEN IT HAS A WINTER COLD?

—FISH-UES!

Which of Santa's reindeer plays basketball?

—Hoop-id!

What is Christmas wrapping paper's favorite sport?

-Bow-ling!

What do you call a holiday dance?

-A snow ball!

What does a snowman put on a Christmas cake?

—Ice-ing!

What was the snowman's favorite year in school?

—Frost grade!

WHAT GOES, "HO, HO, WHOOSH! HO, HO, WHOOSH!"?

—SANTA WEARING CORDUROYS!

Teacher: Tom, recite the alphabet!

Tom: A, B, C, D, E, F, G, H, I, J, K, M, N, O, P, Q, R, S, T, U, V, W, X, Y, Z!

Teacher: You forgot a letter!

Tom: Noel, noel!

WACKY WINTER!

Which winter sport do trees participate in?

-Al-pine skiing!

What is Tarzan's favorite Christmas carol?

–"Jungle Bells!"

Who has antlers, pulls Santa's sleigh, and is really smart?

–A Brain-deer!

What looks like a reindeer, acts like a reindeer, and has antlers like a reindeer?
—A reindeer!

WHAT CRAWLS ON A REINDEER'S HEAD?

—ANT-LERS!

What do you call Santa Claus when his clothes are all wrinkled?

—Kris Krinkle!

YOE!

What kind of cookies do birds leave out for Santa?

—Chocolate chirp!

What did the girl Christmas present say to the boy Christmas present?

—"You're my beau!"

What do you put on a Christmas tree that's on a diet?

—Lites!

CHRISTMAS CAROL
+ MONEY
―――――――――
JINGLE BILLS!

What can't you find at the North Pole?

-The South Pole!

WHAT IS A SNOWMAN'S FAVORITE FOOD?

-CHILI!

Why are Santa's helpers so confident?
-They have good elf-esteem!

Why was Blitzen sad?
-He heard that Christmas comes but once a deer!

Which of Santa's reindeer was a U.S. President?

—Nixen!

WACKY WINTER!

What's more fun than tobogganing?

—Three-bogganing!

What is a cheerleader's favorite Christmas carol?

-"Jingle Yells!"

WHAT DOES SAINT NICK CALL HIS CLOTHES AFTER SLIDING DOWN THE CHIMNEY?

—HIS SANTA CLAUS SOOT!

WOOKY PRESENTS!

What do you call a computer that's shaped like your mouth?

—A lip top!

What do you call a doll that stings?

—Bar-bee!

What musical instrument is a present you can also use to catch fish?

—A clari-net!

What do you call a tool that you can also use to do math problems?

—Multi-pliers!

What do you call a stuffed animal that's not much fun to play with?

—A teddy bore!

What do you call a motorcycle that makes you throw up?

—A Hurley-Davidson!

What do you call a pair of jeans that ring?

—Bell bottoms!

What is white, porcelain, and fun to play with?

—A toy-let!

Where does Santa keep all his red suits?

—In the Claus-et!

WHAT DO ELVES PLAY SOLITAIRE WITH?

—CHRISTMAS CARDS!

What can't you have
after Christmas
dinner?
            –Christmas lunch!

Where does a hunter kiss his girlfriend on Christmas?

            –Under the moose-letoe!

$$\frac{\text{REINDEER} + \text{COW}}{\text{SLEIGH BULLS!}}$$

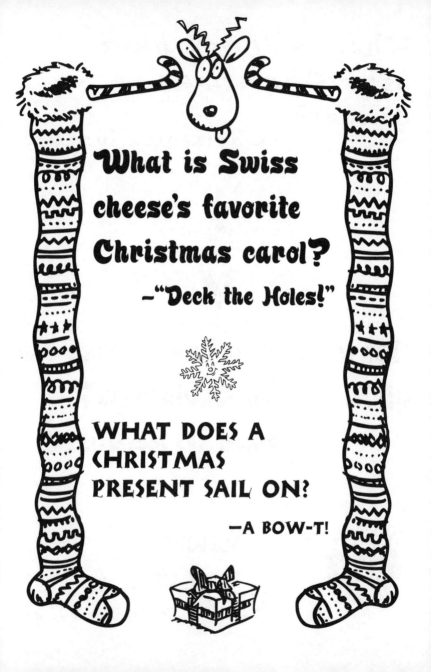

What is Swiss cheese's favorite Christmas carol?

—"Deck the Holes!"

WHAT DOES A CHRISTMAS PRESENT SAIL ON?

—A BOW-T!

What do you call a reindeer
with an attitude problem?
—Rude-olph!

What happened when Santa's
sleigh broke down?

-He had to have it mistle-towed!

What does a baby say on
January 1st?

-"Happy Goo Year!"

**WHAT DOES A SNOWMAN
ORDER AT A FAST FOOD
RESTAURANT?**

-AN ICEBERG-ER!

Why didn't Santa's helper give his friend any Christmas presents?

-Because he was acting s-elf-ish!

Where does a sheep shop for Christmas presents?

-Wool-Mart!

What do you call a really weird Christmas fair?

-A Christmas Bizarre!

What do you call people
who are afraid of Santa?

—Claus-trophobic!

Who has antlers, pulls
Santa's sleigh, and
thinks everything is
about him?

—A Vain-deer!

What does a flower child say on January 1st?

-"Hippie New Year!"

YOE!

WHAT KIND OF AIRCRAFT DOES SANTA FLY AROUND IN?

-A HOLLY-COPTER!

What Christmas plant is really rude?

—Point-settias!

WHAT DOES A JANITOR STRING UP TO DECORATE HIS CHRISTMAS TREE?

—MOP-CORN!

CHRISTMAS CAROL
+ A DOZEN FLOWERS
THE TWELVE DAISIES OF CHISTMAS!

Loon: What did you get for Christmas?

Goon: Yule never guess!

Why was the Christmas goose frowning?

-He was a little down!

What animal shouldn't you invite to a parade?

-A rain-deer!

WHAT DOES SANTA USE WHEN HE NEEDS HELP WALKING?

-A CANDY CANE!

What song does a shopper sing on December 25th?

-"Deck the Malls!"

What is your foot's favorite part of Christmas?

-The mistle-toe!

What is a cow's favorite Christmas carol?

-"Jingle Bulls!"

What is a mallard's favorite Christmas carol?

-"Duck the Halls!"

WHAT ANIMAL MAKES SANTA YAWN?

-A POLAR BORE!

What is a politician's favorite Christmas carol?

-"I'm Dreaming of a White House Christmas!"

WACKY WINTER!

What does a snowman comb his hair with?

-A snowbrush!

WHAT DID THE CHRISTMAS PRESENT WEAR TO THE HOLIDAY DANCE?

-A BOW TIE!

What does Santa Claus eat for breakfast?

-Snow flakes!

What did Santa say to the dry cleaner when he picked up his laundry?

-"Suits me!"

Why did the karate instructor admire Santa?

-Because he has a black belt!

What is a boat's favorite part of the holidays?

-When all the stores have sails!

WHO DELIVERS PRESENTS TO DOGS ON CHRISTMAS?

—SANTA PAWS!

What does Frankenstein buy
for his friends at Christmas?
—Shocking stuffers!

Why are Christmas trees good at sewing?

-They have a lot of needles!

What is Dracula's favorite part of Christmas?

-Santa's vein-deer!

Why are green and red the colors of Christmas?

-Because it's a Holly-day!

What would Albert Einstein use to pull his sleigh if he were Santa Claus?

-Brain-deer!

What do boats say to each other on December 25th?

-"Ferry Christmas!"

Why shouldn't you tell a pig what you got your sister for Christmas?

—Because he'll squeal!

WHAT DO YOU GIVE AN ARTISTIC DOG FOR CHRISTMAS?

—FETCH-A-SKETCH!

WHICH OF SANTA'S REINDEER RUNS IN MARATHONS?

—DASHER!

What carol do you sing after you spend a lot of money on Christmas presents?

—"Jingle Bills!"

What do construction workers use to block traffic in winter?

-Snow cones!

TELLING SANTA YOUR WISHES
+ COMPUTER
―――――――――――――――
SANTA'S LAP-TOP!

@MAD ADD JOKE!

What wears a red and white suit, has a white beard, and loves peanuts?

-Santa Elephant!

What instrument did the fish play at the Christmas concert?

–Bass!

What are red and green and grow on the ocean floor?

–Christmas corals!

WHY DID SANTA HIRE THE NEW SUPERVISOR FOR HIS WORKSHOP?

-HE WAS AN ELF-STARTER!

What do you call the billiard table in Santa's workshop?

-The North Pool table!

What would a sailor leave for Santa to eat?

-Milk and chocolate ship cookies!

What do you call a bunch of trumpets hanging from a pine tree?

-Christmas horn-aments!

WHAT'S COLD AND WHITE AND GOES ON YOUR FOOT?

-A SNOW-SHOE-MAN!

THE 25TH OF DECEMBER
+ A GIRL'S NAME

CHRISTMAS CAROL!

What do you call Santa when he cuts himself shaving?

-Saint Nicked!

What kind of car did the sheep get his wife for Christmas?

-A B-ewe-ick!

Who has antlers, pulls Santa's sleigh, and looks like a lion?

-A Mane-deer!

What is a seamstress' favorite part of Christmas?

-The mistle-sew!

WHICH OF SANTA'S REINDEER COMES FROM PARIS?

-FRANCER!

What's little, has six legs, and says, "Ho, ho, ho!"?

-S-ant-a!

Why did the crab get coal for Christmas?

-Because he was being shellfish!

Why was the pig in such a tizzy?
—There were only three slopping days left until Christmas!

What do you call it when Sir Lancelot visits you on Christmas Eve?

—The Knight Before Christmas!

SANTA CLAUS: HOW DO YOU SPELL CHRISTMAS BACKWARDS?

MRS. CLAUS: C-H-R-I-S-T-M-A-S B-A-C-K-W-A-R-D-S!

WACKY WINTER!

What does a ghost wear to keep his feet warm in winter?

-Booo-ts!

How do you say "Merry Christmas" in Russian?

-"Merry Christmas in Russian!"

What should you name a baby that's born on Christmas?

-Carol!

What did the package say to the bow on Christmas?

-"Quit ribbon on me!"

Who has antlers, pulls Santa's sleigh, and works in construction?

-A Crane-deer!

Why did the snowman put his friend on hold?

-He had coal-waiting!

What does a dog string up to decorate his Christmas tree?

-Pup-corn!

WHERE DO MOST FISHERMEN COME FROM?

-THE NORTH POLE!

Why do birds fly south for the winter?

-Because it's too far to walk!

What does a podiatrist like to do in winter?

-Go toe-bogganing!

What did the ghost wear on his head to keep warm?

-A shocking cap!

What did the snow say as it was melting?

-"It's been ice knowing you!"

Which day of the year is a roof's favorite?
-Christmas Eaves!

When does Santa bring a toad his presents?
-One froggy Christmas Eve!

WHERE DOES SANTA BUILD TOY BOATS?

-IN HIS WORK-SHIP!

WHAT DO YOU GET WHEN YOU CROSS A MUFFLER WITH A DOG?

-A SC-ARF!

What did one SUV give the other SUV on December 25th?

-A Christmas car-d!

WACKY WINTER!

Which winter sport do hairdressers play?

-Curling!

Knock-knock!
Who's there?
Aretha!
Aretha who?
Aretha is hanging
on my door!

What do kids ride to
school in winter?

-Their b-ice-cycles!

**WHO HAS ANTLERS, PULLS
SANTA'S SLEIGH, AND HAS A
REALLY, REALLY BAD HEADACHE?**

-A PAIN-DEER!

What did one Christmas log
say to the other?

-"It's not all about yule!"

Why did the boy have cold feet?

-Because he had snow shoes!

What did the librarian ask Rudolph?

-"Red any good books lately?"

What's the best day
to drink egg nog?
-On the thirst day
of Christmas!

What's the best
day to give a watch
as a present?
-On the second day
of Christmas!

What's the best day
to give golf clubs
as a present?
-On the fore-th day
of Christmas!

What part of your body can you use to wrap Christmas presents?

–Your el-bow!

Who's jolly and merry and brings presents to crows at Christmas?

–Santa Caws!

What does a foot wrap his Christmas presents in?

–Ti-shoe paper!

What's the angriest winter sport?

–Cross-country skiing!

WHAT DO YOUR PUPILS DO IN WINTER?

–THEY GO EYE SKATING!

How does Santa get into a Mexican restaurant?

–He goes down the chimichanga!

KOOKY PRESENTS!

What gives light, has cool liquid in it, and turns into a butterfly?

— A larva lamp!

What present tastes minty and glues your mouth shut?

— Tooth-paste!

What's a haunted present for a camper?

— A creepy teepee!

What is made of gold and sounds like a pig?

— An oink-le bracelet!

What do you call a machine
you can do
math problems
on and get
milk from?

—A cow-culator!

What is round, orange, and cries
a lot?

—A basket-bawl!

What has computer games on it and is
always wandering around?

—A CD roam!

What has a keyboard, a monitor, and a
really bad odor?

—A com-p.u.-ter!

WACKY WINTER!

What do you call your mother's sister in winter?

–Auntie Freeze!

What does one business person say to the other business person on Christmas?

–"Season's Meetings!"

What is the best vegetable to eat in winter?

-Cucum-brrrrrs!

Yoe!

Which winter sport do math teachers participate in?

-Figure skating!

WHAT DID THE DUCK FAMILY HAVE AFTER CHRISTMAS?

-A LOT OF BILLS!

Who did Adam ask to the holiday dance?

-Christmas Eve!

Where does a male hang his Christmas stocking?

-On *the* man-*tle!*

Where does a female hang her Christmas stocking?

-On the woman-tle!

Loon: Did you hear the one about the man who got hit with an icicle?

Goon: Yeah, snow joke!

Why didn't the frozen water go to school?

—It was feeling ice-sick-le!

What do you get when you cross a snowman with a vampire?

-Frost-bite!

What do you get when you cross a reindeer with an insect?

-Ant-lers!

Where does Christmas come before Halloween?
–In the dictionary!

WHAT IS A CHEF'S FAVORITE PART OF CHRISTMAS?
–SEASON'S GR-EAT-INGS!

What does a taxi driver wear
around his neck in winter?

-A s-car-f!

What do kids at the
North Pole write their
Christmas list with?

-Pen-guins!

What do you get when you
cross a chicken with Christmas?

-Feather Christmas!

What did Santa call his pet rabbit?

-Santa's Little Hopper!

What does Mrs. Claus call Santa when he has a cold?
-Snot Nicholas!

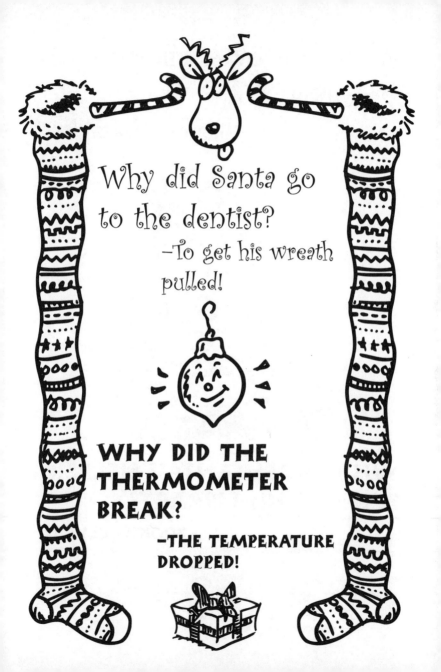

Why did Santa go to the dentist?
—To get his wreath pulled!

WHY DID THE THERMOMETER BREAK?
—THE TEMPERATURE DROPPED!

What does Swiss cheese say on December 25th?

–"Happy Hole-idays!"

WHAT DOES SANTA'S HELPER HAVE IN HIS LIBRARY?

–BOOKSH-ELVES!

What winter sport do computer geeks play?

-Hack-ey!

What did Santa's helpers say at Christmas dinner?

-"Elf yourself!"

Where does a snowman keep his money?

-In a snow bank!

What is Santa's favorite donut?

-Bear claus!

Why was the computer so quiet on Christmas Eve?

–Not a creature was stirring, not even a mouse!

WACKY WINTER!

Which Olympics do victorious people play in?

-The Win-ter Olympics!

What do Santa's helpers do to work out their problems?

-They go to an elf-help group!

What clears snowy roads, has an udder, and says, "Moo"?

-A snow cow!

MUSICAL INSTRUMENT
+ REINDEER
ORGAN DONNER!

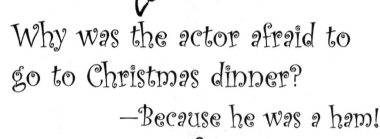

Why was the actor afraid to go to Christmas dinner?

—Because he was a ham!

What does Little Miss Muffet mail to her friends at the holidays?

—Christmas curds!

HAPPY NEW YEAR

What does a postcard say on January 1st?

–"Happy View Year!"

What does a boyfriend say on January 1st?

–"Happy Woo Year!"

What did the ladder do on January 1st?

–He rung in the new year!

What does an owl say on January 1st?

–"Happy Hoo Year!"

What does a dog say on January 1st?

–"Happy Doo Year!"

What does a basketball player say on January 1st?

–"Hoop-y New Year!"

What does a bunny say on January 1st?

–"Hop-y New Year!"

What does a pile of dirt say on January 1st?

–"Heap-y New Year!"

What does Frankenstein say on January 1st?

–"Happy New Fear!"

What's the best day to give a horn as a present?

—On the sax day of Christmas!

What's the best day to eat a Christmas feast?

—On the ate-th day of Christmas!

What's the best day to go camping for the holidays?

—On the tent-th day of Christmas!

What do reindeer plant in the fall?

-Christmas bulbs!

What does Santa take when he has a cold?

-A North Pill!

What does Kris Kringle do to relax?

-He goes to the Sauna Claus!

Who has antlers, pulls Santa's sleigh, and is really, really messy?

-A Stain-deer!

What did Donner say when Blitzen told him a joke?

-"You sleigh me!"

What is the least fun winter sport?

-Snow-bored-ing!

What does a golfer hate to eat for Christmas dinner?

—A slice of ham!

What do you call the Stooges at the North Pole?

—Larry, Curly, and Eski-mo!

What is a kid's favorite Christmas carol?

—"Toy to the World!"

Why was the snowman always forgetting things?

-He was flaky!

WHAT DID SANTA SAY WHEN HE BUILT A SKI RESORT?

-"I'M MAKING A LIFT, I'M CHECKING IT TWICE!"

HOW DID THE DETECTIVE FIND THE STOLEN CHRISTMAS TREE?

–HE LOOKED FOR SANTA CLUES!

What do you get when you combine hot sauce with a Christmas bow?

–Barbeque rib-bons!

Where does a dog shop
for Christmas presents?
—Wal-Mutt!

Where does Santa vote?

—The North Poll!

What did Santa say when
Mrs. Claus didn't want to go
down the chimney with him?

—"Soot yourself!"

WACKY WINTER!

What did they say to the Olympic sledder when he came in last?

-"You're such a luge-er!"

What should someone with bad breath eat after Christmas dinner?

-Mints-meat pie!

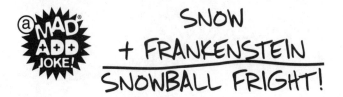

SNOW
+ FRANKENSTEIN
SNOWBALL FRIGHT!

WHY DOES EVERYONE ENJOY DECEMBER?

–BECAUSE IT'S A WIN-WINTER SITUATION!

What does Santa
use to line his
cabinets?
          -Sh-elf paper!

What is Mr. & Mrs.
Claus' kid called?
          -Son-ta!

What did the omelet say
on December 25th?

          -"Merry Eggs-mas!"

SANTA'S HELPERS
+ CIRCUS ANIMAL
AN ELF-ANT !

WHAT DO YOU CALL A FLEA IN SANTA'S BEARD?

—SAINT NICHO-LOUSE!

What should you say to a snowman when he's mad?

–"Chill out!"

What is a snowman's favorite song?

–"There's No Business Like Snow Business!"

What does a sorcerer
write at Christmas?
                    –A witch list!

What did the gift say
when the teacher
took attendance?
                    –"Present!"

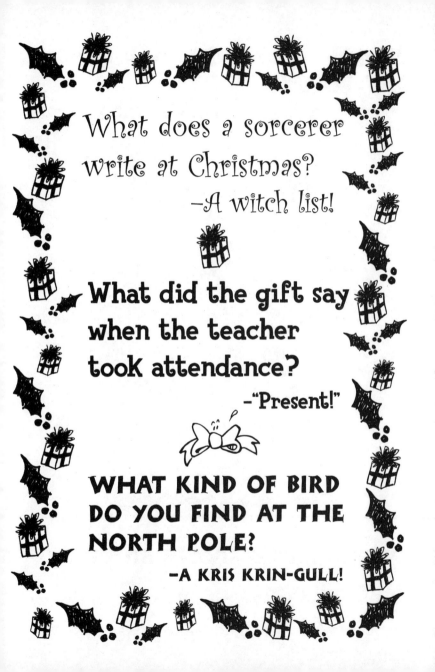

WHAT KIND OF BIRD
DO YOU FIND AT THE
NORTH POLE?
                    –A KRIS KRIN-GULL!

WHAT DID SANTA CALL HIS PET PUPPY?

-SANTA'S LITTLE YELPER!

Yoe!

What does a snowman put on Christmas cookies?

-Frost-ing!

Where does a bodybuilder kiss his girlfriend on Christmas?

-Under the muscle-toe!

Why is winter so much fun?

-You have a snow ball!

What do chickens do at Christmas?

—Eggs-change gifts!

WHAT DO YOU CALL A KANGAROO AT THE NORTH POLE?

—LOST!

What is a store clerk's
favorite Christmas carol?

-"Jingle Sells!"

What do you put on your
turkey at Christmas dinner?

-Seasonings Greetings!

WHERE DOES AN OYSTER KISS HIS GIRLFRIEND ON CHRISTMAS?

-UNDER THE MUSSEL-TOE!

What does Santa wear on his head to keep warm?

-A polar ice cap!

When does Santa bring a toad his presents?

-One froggy Christmas Eve!

Why did all of the other reindeer laugh?

-Because they were reading this book!